The Green Dress Whose Girl is Sleeping

Jocelyn

'in defiance, feed us!

15/10/15

The Green Dress Whose Girl is Sleeping

Russell Jones

FREIGHT BOOKS

First published 2015
By Freight Books
49-53 Virginia Street
Glasgow, G1 1TS
www.freightbooks.co.uk

A CIP catalogue reference for this book is available from the British Library.

ISBN 978-1-910449-37-0

Typeset by Freight in Meta Serif
Printed and bound by Bell and Bain, Glasgow

the publisher acknowledges investment from
Creative Scotland toward the publication of this book

MC

Contents

My Secrets as a God

Whoever says omnipotence is good
is as bad as his word. Truth is I've seen
too much. I've watched deserts flood,
cities tumble, women burn, I've stood
with the kind, the godly, the downright mean.

When civilisations charged into battle
I was necessary, I was there, I was the gleam
and the darkness on their mantle,
a dead man's word, hallucinatory babble,
his flash of white, his nightmare, his dark dream.

I've secrets I'm bound to keep and yet
there's nothing of you that I've not gleaned,
heard, felt. I know you, your loss, regrets,
the sting of your love, how you begged to forget
that smell, that silent sun, so you changed routine.

If there's something I could pray for
I'd choose confession: that velvet screen
between us. I'd whisper the door
down, call it a miracle. And more
than anything I would ask for your forgiveness.

God Has Still Not Appeared to the Birds

In Boston we kept a jar
of eggs, thought nothing
of the life

cracked onto the waffle iron.
This palm shook, rattled out
a yolk. At the window

starlings – I think they were –
flew by us. Do you think
they saw

my shudder, my shell,
my hands? A knuckle
remembers

the old wounds it gave,
the eggs it's beaten
and God

has still not appeared
to the birds. These hands
are my knives, my gut,

they have tasted things.
Think about that
chick

that hit the *thud* window
like a wet sponge and let out
its first

and final choke of a song.
These hands
took it,

they have felt things
breathe, life flap
in the smallest wings.

Apparition in a Storm

There's a speck on your tail
that might say something

about you. We're in the daisies,
next to no daffodils, waiting

for the clouds to pass
across us, between us.

Are you watching too?
We twitch, we perch

by that towering statue
and the world is falling.

Watch the leaf tumble,
the breeze die. What an air

to throw. You ask for the earth
to break and it does.

I'll stay with you, then,
as the statue

is painted darker by the rain
for a darker world.

There Wasn't Anybody Else

Just that one silhouette, man-shaped
and calling out to the spit-slick ocean.
No-one would hear what he might
have said, his resident voice.
He sent it out, a hopeless dinghy
in a hurricane, cracked mast, tangled rope.
No-one would hear him explain
the tilt of his tongue that groped
the buck of his teeth, the dirty wash.
He wanted silence, or the brush
of the water's song, or his yelp
to mingle with the outdoors;
to soak frustration, drown a temper,
skim love about like a pebble.
Just that one silhouette, man-shaped
until morning; then just one voice.

The Insider

The sun comes before the morning
and a man puts the ground to his ear.

At the party the green dress dances
so wild that her hips shake the atmosphere.

Our songs are rising as our dead crumble
back into the earth where we lose them.

And the morning sun lights up the sequins
of the green dress whose girl is sleeping.

The Chase

Where the point and the surface meet: this is how I think
of her as she crosses the street, hand in her bag, foot
from the floor, a real torpedo. When our eyes hanker for
proximity like the poles of a magnet, I know I'm beat. She
darts behind a two storey bus, other-worldly for that brief
acceleration, and is mine again. My legs can carry the city's
grace, the National Gallery, the chirp of a starling in one
stride and within twenty I'm beside her, looking at her,
seeing through her. *What do you want?* she asks, the wind
on her tongue. *You,* I say as my breath meets hers.

My Adoration of Tiramisu

When the evening curls by and the streets shush,
when I think of unfolding from beneath you
towards the kitchen, fingering your lips to a hush;
when I turn from your eyes and those few
noisy glances, when you reconsider
where our romance is

I'll return with spoons
and, tuneless, place one quiet bowl before us.
I will wrap my words and whispers around.
I'll be kind, I will be generous
and even when we envy the ease of sound
I will resist and, in defiance, feed us.

Salvage crew

Won't you remember me
in the garden, the bright birds
bending the sky
toward us?

Remember the night our eyes played
on the vista, how our lips flew
in the warm evening

and if you remember the horizon
then place my silhouette
beside you.

The flowers are closing, this day's
roots are withdrawing and we
are the last of the light
on its petals.

That Song

not her swelter, her pinkie   but that song
not her morning breath, her peppermint purse   but that song
not her gravel, her linguini   but that song
not her zane, her overt ordinariness in public   but that song
not her intricate dental routine, her mink   but that song
not her sausage and eggs, her thigh   but that song
not her towel, her unsustainability   but that song
not her one summer shoe, her horizon   but that song
not her teeter, her titter   but that song
not her bargain hunt, her poacher's eyes   but that song
not her quiver, her taste for a good sunrise   but that song
not her, her absence   but that song

girl.drm

Lie back, jack in. This dream is electric,
was my reality and tonight you'll see
it too: the shadow below her,
the phosphorescence that hangs above
my girl can be yours.

You can share her: tongue the ice-cream
from her midriff. Steal her fingertips, suck
the drowsy breath from her lips.
That sand she's lying on for you
was for me. The ocean that absorbs her toes
was from our first summer by the sea.

Dream carefully. When she's curious she smiles,
she avoids apology, never lets on
that she's afraid of the shifting darkness,
the cold breeze. She is a phantom
of memory but you will never know
her outside this moment, so remember

as my mind drifts,
as my vision closes,
so will yours.

The Bang

Alice and Atlas:
Opposing Protons in the Large Hadron Collider

Alice: Pretty naked, pretty fast. For the sake of staying positive, call me Alice.

Atlas: *< flexing his quarks>* And me, Atlas.

Alice: Pleased to meet you at last. So this is magnetism. Can I ask –

Atlas: Oh baby, do.

Alice: What are we doing here? For what cause?

Atlas: We're on course.

Alice: Yes, but for what? To charge? To sing? To spin?

Atlas: The truth is in the name. Not Hadron, but Collider. We're set for, done for.

Alice: But we've this time at least. *<Enthused, charged>* How romantic!

Atlas: Well let's be quick about it.

Alice: Can we kiss?

Atlas: We can collide.

Alice: Has it always been? You seem something of an opportunist.

Atlas: I am.

Alice: It's not how I dreamt it, but I admit the motion
         takes me.

Atlas: Come closer, my sweet Alice.

*<Atlas and Alice approach each other at 299.8 million metres
per second>*

Alice: I'm split; Atlas, I'm not sure I've anything for you.

Atlas: I adore you.

Alice: Well, perhaps –

Atlas: Perhaps?

Alice: Perhaps.

Chromosome Medley

2052 - choices for the unconceived

Baby blue or baby brown as Bombay
mix, bark, a chest of drawers.

What's hereditary? Remove the walrus
from the walrus. Your mother's snout

needn't be yours. Here, take this flawless
mandible, push the outy inny, avoid

that fleshy, cankerous, cancerous brick
gifted by daddy. Who said God?

Every choice made for us
is every choice made for us.

1984 – one case example

Dad shaves, showers in cologne,
doesn't comb his hair for fashion.

Mum shaves, washes her hair,
detonates her eyelashes.

Dad drives, drinks, walks, jokes,
uses his one chat-up line on complexion.

Mum walks, drinks, sings, smokes,
eyes, trousers her way to conception.

0008 – the human race

Tongue-quick, word-quick, spermatozoa-quick,
a thousand generations bang their head

on a charged urethra. Carry the messages
of ancestry, little single-cell, carry

the burden and the brilliance of homosapientry
and plant it deep as the corpses, wide as the world.

A light of life flickers like a first word,
two caveats merge, two eyes piece together

under the auditorium. Darkness cannot determine
the bright mind but the dull sound - thrump thrump -

of war drums, the gentle burn of morning song
can. And food is what feeds: a yearning

for crushed grass, charcoal, daisy petals,
a hen's carcass, peas. There aren't always choices

but there are always decisions. The baby won't be born
with a book but it may still read.

The blue eye may be clearer
than the brown but both will see.

In the Classroom

Children are gods too.
In this room one teenager stands
and cracks his knuckles through
long division, puts his hand

up, asks to be let out.
He leaves, quite calm, for a quiet
minute, then screams *FUCK IT*.
The class are on the verge of riot

and no-noise-astonishment.
I let them blether,
call for management,
pull myself together.

This morning
his dad didn't come back
again. Mum was smoking
her last brick, told her son *That prick*

better no come back, ken,
I'll do him in. When the boy was six
– he stayed with gran then –
he was a fuck, a fix

for someone, no name,
says the report we have squeezed
in our filing cabinet. He's taken home,
mum's gone, but he has the keys.

Random Sample from the School Career Library Classification Index

Dairy worker
Dietician
Diamond cutter
Design technician

Offshore rigger
Oral advisor
Organic gardener
Organiser

Lane sweeper
Librarian
Lighthouse keeper
Linguist: Bulgarian

Educator
Estimator
Explosives expert
Exterminator

The First Kiss

What a disappointment. Nothing like the movies,
nothing like the mind. A mass of muscles writhing,
an awkward hand on a tightened arse
at the under-sixteens "Angel and Demon Night"

What a farce. Is this the limbo
stick for life? Where are the fireworks,
the butterflies, the butterflies exploding
like fireworks into a glorious rainbow
of wings and ash?

My son will sit with me and I'll tell him
the truth that there is no word to fit
a feeling of lust and immediate unrest.
Or the lingering taste, the pleasure, the alien
of a first kiss. There's no word, I'll tell him,
for the particular fullness that breaks through
the lungs and fills you with the breath
of their hair, for the sudden rush of two hands
clambering until the fingers find
each other and grip. Grip to that, I'll tell him
and be thankful for the imperfection
of love and that the first kiss is nothing
like you expected.

Lament for a Lost Son

    my boss visits her son's grave
    every night, lights a candle
in his memory
    in her memory

    I watch as she punches
    holes, stacks papers,
parts of her
    in the cemetery

    the dead, like so many
    rays of light
have passed
    through our fingers

Haunting

It's only in you that I re-live,
re-die at my roadside
on loop, round about,
like a campaign video.
Don't maintain the vigil
to prove something: that the dying

morning must take you with it.
Those garage bouquets stringed
to the lamppost, that headstone
is not me. I am nothing like the everlasting
white noise of my life,
the thought of my body lifting
and lifting and falling over
a car bonnet at midnight. I am not a placard,
a rainbow, a respirator, I am not
a mound. You are one of many
in their homes, a decade of parents poring
over the vistas, longing for something
more than the shadows to return
in the red evening. Let that pass.
Those bodies of memory are just
memories of the body, straggling

fawns at a dead end.
Don't think so negative,
so photographic. Do not think of me
as unmade, unkissed, unchanging,
unfaltering, unhated, unloved.

Heading to the Corner Shop on a Winter's Day

The air shattered
in a scream which I followed, pounding,
and found a woman lying
snow-angel still on the ice
repeating, half choking, half heaving,
my baby, my baby –

Two men lifted her forward, slowly
unfastened the sling from her shoulders, held her
away from the crushed sack of limbs
as we telephoned.

It was something none of us could take
or leave, so we stood
together, separate
in a limbo of stillness and dread
until the useless immediacy of the ambulance arrived
and we were relieved.

Towers

What they came for

not answered by the hurricane

The machine that defied

the gravity of belief

the panes and concrete

still as the dust outruns

in a hotel room, nursing

for a latte bought a day earlier

Now he has it tacked to his office door

but pass it and remember

of paper that escaped

is another question

of the explosion.

humanity,

smashes through

like water. A globe stands

the feet. My dad sits

his sick wife and a receipt

from the top floor cafe.

so he can't help

those burning flocks

the high windows

Sendai-shi

Sachie will still marry; her children will see
her past through the family album
that she will keep wrapped in linen,
bring out on occasion. She will pore over
her life with them, the places that are gone,
the days she spent growing by the sea
that are now taken by it, and those that were
ripped away by the wave. She will stream
through the blur that is her life in Sendai,
the green city whose ghosts are forever drowning
under the households of the tsunami.
Her children will read about it in school textbooks
and in their mother's face, they will see
the sorrow running through her slowly wash away
as the city regrows, recovers and learns to live on.

The Forest

The city and its people are locked together,
not in monuments or stone effigies,
not in the solid slab of steps and spires,
not in newly furnished apartment blocks
but in sound, earthly noise. They come together
like a web of roots, a radical spread, a flurry of leaves
urging growth, together in the timbre of one tune,
one voice, one trunk armoured by the bark of many.

When a tree falls and thousands are there
to hear it, it makes a sound: cast out the saw
for song. If we refuse to be pierced then show us
the vibration of the air we defy; the slow, low hum
rising like a flock of wood pigeons
at the crack of a gun. Watch the ground
fly and the branches shatter. We will reek
of its sap and taste the oil of the upheaval.

Night Camp

There we were in the goat's field,
you checking for ticks and me guessing
at good wood for midnight's fire,
our sun withering as we pelted ahead
with the final preparations:
to put four posters under the sky.

We took the timber saw between us,
held it tight along the oldest tree we could find.
Back and forward, perfectly synchronised,
spitting dust. By its last creak, night was nearly on us.

You pulled the mattress from the undergrowth,
arms rippling in the half-moon. I climbed barefoot
and brought down the blankets of canopy.
We stood in the absolute darkness of the country,
drafted a fire, stripped down to nothing but shadows.

Fastening the drapes around us we lay back
on the dying ferns, tiny insect eyes
probing from the frame as we slipped,
still, between dreams.

Breathing Space

Stars, don't start.
Leave me to everything.
Burn away. Your glimmers
have made their point
though it's lost.

Let me freewheel
in your distant light,
handstanding, vaulting
through the folds
of your surveillance.

If we'd wanted to see you
every minute of every night
we'd not have built houses,
built factories to drab your sky.
This is our canopy, our cloth
between your vastness
and the immediate universe
of our eyes.

OUR TERRACED HUM

Studio, 4 a.m.

She has the quickness of the hour: pot purged,
brush brandished before sunrise. What wrath!
What ferocious speed! What power! Submerged
in the curtain of night she postures, laughs,
aglow, her head thrown back apropos.
She watches the paint dry. In the morning
she will rise, shower, butter toast and go
to work. She will bake bread in the evening,
run a bath for her children, please her man.
Which of us has the canvas for dreaming?
I sit watching the lives of others, fan
whirring, reeling in the sweaty cling
of life. Our terraced hum is an echo
heard vicariously through the shadows.

The Flat Opposite

He watches the television at night,
absorbed as she strolls behind him
cradling a dozen tea-candles, alight
in the washroom. She sets them on the rim
of a drawn bath, steam silhouetting her
in the frost of the jarred window. She strips,
the small lights dancing on her skin, a blur
of dreams as she arches, lowers her hips,
breasts and neck beneath the surface. One hour
passes without consequence until she blows
out the flames and dresses in the flowers
of white smoke. She stops at the door, frozen,
flawless. He flicks through channels as though
he's never seen the goddess through my window.

Basement Beneath the Corner Shop

He's made himself the castle of his dreams:
the landfill lord, a tin can Midas
moated by nine months of debris. He beams
in the grit of his homemade fortress
because nothing outside can finger through
the pizza-box walls cracked by arrow loops,
his cardboard curtain. The hullaballoo
of reality is cut by his coup
d'état, cartons stacked, wrappers tacked, intact
in the order of chaos. Passersby
gleer in, hands fanned over their eyes, retract,
shake their faces at the teem of house flies.
They mark him the idol of their own disgust
when in public but, privately, they lust.

Garden State

Old guy finds peace in posies, a tall mug
of whisky. He kneels with his eyes screwed shut,
nostrils wide as roses; surrounded, rug
to hearth to ceiling, by wildflowers cut
that morning. What a state he's built himself
from Aaron's Rod, Allgood, Adam's Needle,
Alexander's Black Lovage, Aneth.
A mass of gnomes sit in this wild city, all
facing him as though he is their god,
rod-hands together in prayer. A light smacks
the lord, grows bright, burning, blinding, good.
Then he smiles, naked chest sculpted, bold, black
and one knowing eye winks as our worlds swim
in the rainbow of life that surrounds him.

Above the "100% Human Hair Extensions" Beauty Salon

We could never call those eyes listless, boy,
at the speed they study the streets : hot rod
bawling down the road and into the sky,
a gaggle of drunks who whoop at girls,
singing brotherhood hymns from the football grounds.
What angels those pigeons make through your mind,
trash glittering in great whirls of colour,
painted hurricanes that wake and whizz.
The clamorous reek of a chip supper
and road fumes ignite in the breath
of a dragon that soars, flips and roars.
You clamber onto her back, right leg
following left, stroking her well worn
wings as you whisper your destination –

Open Window, Toilet Room Suicide

Is it ill instinct that grasps this one gull?
An open port is too much to resist.
He staggers across the sill in full
view, colony screeching. Is it a twist
of nature that takes his sharp foot inside?
He ponders the sink as he walks the tiles.
He takes to the toilet to check the tide:
still as clockwork. Is it vastness, the miles
of flight that make the saltwater so sweet?
The routine is tested, ancient and wise.
He leaps to the cistern, surveys the seat,
yanks the chain with his beak. He drowns the cries
outside, screeching, swirling on a throne
of wild cataracts until he is gone.

The Call

They are not back yet. She hovers over
the hob, half-dancing. Is it the telephone?
She moves to answer. Takes the receiver.
She says hello. Yes. She sits down, moans,
puts a hand over her eyes, breathes, shakes.
The handset's wet, she yanks it from the wall,
slams it on the kitchen table. It breaks.
She is silent for a long moment, bawls
until her eyes and lips are raw. She stops.
She stands and takes a knife from the side drawer,
a loaf from the cupboard, butter. She drops
what she's doing to clear the phone from the floor.
The front door opens and her boys enter.
She smiles, greets them and serves the dinner.

Study, Siblings

He's on the top rung, her on tippytoes:
sprites of possession hauling their mother's
tomes to the floor. They lay them out in rows
of fascination: *Pickling for Larders,*
Advanced Mathematics for Beginners,
A History of the World, Spring Seeding,
Plato's Question, The Good Home: A Winner's
Guidebook to Genetic Engineering.
But the ache of the child is in design:
they clasp the pages between them and pull
leaves from limb, shred the sheets from their spine.
In the mirage of devastation all
pages swarm as one. Through this new release
they revel in the wholeness of the pieces.

Loft Conversion, The Smoking Gallery

His cigar smoke lingers like the old ghost
of his gun, whose muzzle shot the jaw off
a red stag in '37. He toasts:
to love and life, to port and sport. His loft
is a haven of eyes in the desert
of a blind city. I watch his glass grind
along the rim of his teeth as he skirts
his tar-nails through the drinks cabinet. Mind
and man meet in the memory
of the chase: an antler, a hoof, a tail
for eternity, for taxidermy.
What forgotten things he finds in a trail
through the hills of youth. But what's undone
remains in the art of preservation.

Reflections on the Dog House

It's too late but summer never lets up:
the stoned streets are bright and brash. We glare
in sweat and silence, each with his nose up
at the bare pane; chimeras in the glare
of one another. That slump of a hound
paws the glass, eyes sacked from the lack of sleep
and the grind of an empty house. I hound
the window and howl, chase my tail, whine. Sleep,
let us dogs lie in a cradle of stars –
we will never again slash up the lounge
or pull on the carpet. We will be stars,
soundless, sated and serene as we lounge
in the diamond of your darkness. Let us
lose the sight of reflection. Please, let us.

Star

nd
hen
din
nding
r a din
dim din
nding dim
im dimmer
nding in a then and then and a din
din ending in a dim din din din
e dim is ending in a dim
art a dim dart again
again dim dimmer
a gain in dints
and in darts
in darts it
starts in
stints in
stints it
starts

nd
1en
din
nding
1 a dln
dim din
nding dim
im dimmer
nding in a then and then and then and a din
din ending in a dim din din din
1e dim is ending in a dim
art a dim dart again
again dim dimmer
a gain in dints
and in darts
in darts it
starts in
stints in
stints it
starts

Gaze

In a glance the night sky recalls
the bright sparks that began
our planet's overture: diamonds
veined through the earth,
blue cheese, a marble floor,
volcanic coughs and iron birds,
a declining sundial, the supernova
that birthed bright pearls of human song.

But it surrenders nothing that is not earned.
Rome rises, swords charge, a leech
suckles, a bed of periwinkles multiplies,
an ape stands for the first time and walks.
And no slim telescope will show it all,

two eyes cannot see a million others,
one man cannot have a million lovers
as one flower does not aspire to be a meadow.

House Plant

She had tomatoes growing
in the living room, too

precious, those fat rubies,
for what nature intended.
You're never to eat them,
she insisted, *never*. So I

didn't, and we watched
them grow like children.
The sunlight made them
lean to the window, leaves

fingering the glass
until the stem bent

under the weight of the fruit,
until those gems broke free
from the purse, scattered,
turned black. We left them,

let them rot on the carpet.
I didn't say a thing,

but I should have, I ought to
have taken the plant out
to know the garden, to let
the whitefly ravish it.

On Waiting for Milk

Lost in the start of this winter morning

through a city fog. Like drums in the snow,

I hear two milk boys come, briskly walking

through a motionless, calcium veil. Now

I hear their bottles turning, I invent

the hunch of their delivery. I create

an image of the duo twice-bent,

lifting a fresh dawn through their milking crate.

Then a change of light: I graze the pathway,

cream my tongue for the voice of morning work,

take a tone for enough bottle to say

something meaningful as they lift and walk.

They pass, hoof-footed, cold and unsurprised.

I say nothing, move nothing, go inside.

26 ONE WORD POEMS

Another Bite and Then the Diet Starts
Appetizer

Boyhood Dream, Male Reality (Unfortunately They're His Own)
Boobs

Chrissy, 48, Loves Cats, Hates Cheaters, Smoker
Cat-as-trophe?

Darlin' It's Not You...
Delusion

ENTER IF YOU DARE!!!
Exit

Folk These Days Don't Know They're Born
Fuddy-duddy

Gravediggings for Breakfast
Granola

Have You Trouble Hearing?
Herring?

Icarus, Fresh from an Afternoon Dreaming, Strode Forward with His Hands in His Pockets, Harked *I've an all-inclusive booked in Majorca, paid on the plastic. Onward!*
Imbecile

Jagged Winter with a Terrifying Spring
Jaberwocky

Kafuffle of Love / Art is Misunderstanding / Death is Song and Dance
Kabuki

Leaves Blow in the Long Wind of Spring
Lenten

Magniiiification
mnmalsm

Nay! Neigh!
Nag

Onomatopoeia Walks Into a Bar: thunk
One-liner

Petite Bundles
Pic can inn ies

Quality Engagement and Wedding Bands at LOW LOW Prices, Mail Order NOW
Quartz

Rolling into an Etch of the Mind
REM

Speaking of Sin
sssssssssssssssssssssex

Tobacco, Tequila and Karaoke Friday
Tracheotomy

Unborn Clings to the Mic
Ultrasound

Versa
Vice

What You See Is What You Get
WYSIWYG

X-Ray Dept./ CT Suite ; Orthopaedic and Fracture ; Males Only Ward
Xanthippe

Yaddah Yaddah Yaddahaaahahaaeeee
Yak

Zealot Packs His Trolley Full of Cold Meats
Zombie

The Woman with a Rabbit Sitting on Her Cardigan

He'll be your mouthful, your pot.
Take him now, cuddle him, say your goodbyes.
The rabbit shuffles as if he knows
that your eyes have designs for him.

Don't shuffle, don't spill your tea.
He knows more than he's letting you know.
See his neck snap like a drawer shuts
on its hinges, his eyes whiten, the pot boil.

Red Squirrel

I watched you find the places hidden by the snow,
dig up those old plots that went remembered.
Diligent, you let the empty spaces go.

The spirit is harder than the soil.
This deep winter is littered with holes.
I've nothing to do, nowhere to go, but with you.

You make a joke, *You must be nuts*. I groan.
But you reveal the secrets of your wild anyway.
There must be something wrong,

I know but I can't change.
You look at the boy I am, underneath,
a lost little thing to put into the ground.

You've put your paw on that, I realise. I take
what we have in my clumsy hands,
shoo you away and rebury it.

The Elephant Wash

They're not elephant enough.
Tusks sawn back, legs chained, led
into the water where they're beaten
to lie, half submerged, islands of flesh
and heads, the occasional eye.

When the washers whip
the elephants' scarred backs
a few of us flinch. We watch
in the reek of dung,
the thick yellow soap is acrid.

An Aussie says *This is old school
animal training*, adjusts
his camera lens, takes a photo
with his kids. The workers thrash
sticks across their trunks,
we're not sure why. They plough
sharpened coconut husks
over and over and over
the rawing fields of skin.
One woman says she's
had enough of this
and leaves.

As we lose interest
we follow the small herd
to the taxi rank
where a shrivelled
grey woman begs,
arm stretched out like a weak trunk,
fingering for our change.

Kingfisher

I was in the 39 degree winter of Kochi.

The water was sleeping,
I was riding on its dream.

Suddenly, led by the changing shadows,
he flashed through the warm breeze,
plummeted into that second world.

He had barely left me
but his dive filled the river.
Not a drop of movement on the surface
but his image hung, ablaze,

his wings like cloaks of energy.
His tail was a bolt of topaz.
His beak was sunlight, mango, flame.
His feet were origami

folded from the backwaters of India
and in his hunter's eyes precision shone.
In the silence, in the centre
of the season he was a vein,

a quick beating rhythm.
He came back empty
but time snapped

and was reborn
in his dance

of light and fire and ice.

Down on the Beach

And now we go in hands,
across the rocks of the coast on toes,
barefoot, eyes down, mouths open,
sucking that sweet salt air.

As we edge the sand we glance up
to the horizon, let out a ghoul
of a cry, so white we seem transparent.
We hold our breaths.

There, by the rotting breaker:
a mass of flesh choking,
gagging, inebriated
on that pitch black surf.

And the sea rolls black
and forward, catching it,
bill wide for air
but filled with that sinister rainbow.

It's almost beautiful in its end,
as the water strips away
its feathers to make a coat
flapping in the wind.

We watch the light die as it fails
to dive, to float, to fly, to fight.
Its robust call wanes under
our slick dark gaze, until
its sharp movements slow,
shake and sink and stop –
beak down, eye wide
and white and we
stand there
watching.

Whale

It has stopped.
It is waiting to make
an island.
It is drifting
at near stillness,
mouth bound,
tongue hung,
blowhole beat.
It is waiting
for you to stroll,
from your boat,
along its back
and think
it is dead.
It will be
a fat corpse.
It will be
flesh.
It will be
what you expect.
You will hum
its deep song
and think
it is harmless.
It is here
to eat
and it will eat.
It is here
to rise
and it will rise.

On Old Fishmarket Close

The old men appear, they know their place,
which fish to sell from their trawler baskets.
They hold them out like their children, mouths gaped
in the humming sun, scales shifting. Look, you'll miss it
if your mind flails, if your gaze swims too much
in the anchor of today. Let their tales, their voices pick
through the bones of history and find you hunched
among the bright, the new, the old and blackened brick.
I am smoking on the porch of a chic cafe,
splashing into anchovy butter, a bundle of bread sticks;
tourists streaming like salmon up the steep throughway
for something to snap, something ancient, unique.
I pack the poem, clear the air, scatty from the salt and smoke,
the fish lingering, old men evaporating, as I leave the close.

Selection from a Summer Set

I

High white emerges,
surf-boy hovers on his board.
Nature is captured.

IV

Cliffs hold the winter
shades near. Birds cross the evening,
slow and silently.

V

A warm sun welcomes
the morning. Schoolboys scatter
like clouds of minnows.

IX

Whale men watch women
for calendar legs. Ice-cream
is reality.

Hunger

In the frequent stumble of a cider night,
homeward, an uneasy rumble grows, a tight

growl. The chippy's closed. The 24 hour petrol shop
has shut down. When'd that happen? I stop

and push my pale face against the Chinese
like an orphaned boy in a Christmas Special. Please

let the Turkish meat emporium be open. No.
I know the curry house is closed for diwali, so

sit in the street, clumsily roll and light
a cigarette to cage the appetite.

A bird pecks at nothing. A man shoos
his dog from my feet. A fat couple enter the public loos

and don't come out for a quarter of an hour.
I piss across a storm-beaten tree. The glower

of time has taken its toll. Can a man
eat a stone? A stick? A half-empty soda can?

I dance to the meadow, where mushrooms grow
and I know there are few poisonous kinds so

pull them up. They give themselves
so easily and I delve

deeper into the forestry, picking up
pace. This woodland is my deli: a buttercup,

a dandelion clock, and under a rock behind a bush
a menagerie of scuttling amuse-bouche

for my eager mouth. I throw them in, incessantly,
their tiny heads popping, bodies throbbing, bobbing in a sea

of yellow blood and saliva. So deep now
I can barely see the tree for the woods, how

the moon fights away the stars, can barely
feel the wind, the night on my skin clearly.

A new spirit takes me: cast away
the blockades of clothing! Today

the sun rises on a new man, a beast, a lark
flying out to meet a new sun, out from the dark.

Cast out that shell of the city and into the new, the now, the stark!
I wake up hours later: 5am, half naked, half hammered,
    in the park.

Apologies to My Body

Body, I'm sorry. Sincerely. I'm sorry
for the pounds of flesh
I put in, put on. I'm sorry
for midnight's sofa, for lying in.
I'm sorry about the beer – I couldn't help
myself. I'm sorry for all the cider, too,
for sherry, vodka, tequila.
Sunrise is something we've seen
too little of and, for that, Body, I apologise.
Body, I'm sorry for our eyes,
that I dismissed the gravity of mountains,
have not set them sailing enough.
Tell the ears that I'm sorry about Hanson's *MmmBop*.
They deserved Rachmaninoff.
Body, I'm sorry for the scars I got as a child,
for the disappointing nights with women I barely knew.
You have been good to me, body, and I've been
 – let's face it – worse to you.
Body, I'm sorry we don't go out more,
that our piano fingers have memorised
the QWERTY keyboard instead of scores.
I'm sorry that exercise became a chore.
When we were seventeen we were pristine.
Body, I'm sorry we only see abdomens in magazines.
But we've time, Body, and heart. I should mention
cigarettes, kebab 'meat', colonic 'upsets', the sweats,
the blues, dry lips, man-tits and, yes, the tattoos.
And love never helped us, did it? It left us
quaking in the dark binge of my room.
But Body, there's something to us,
something flaccid, fragile, something
near-marvellous. Let's go now,
Body, round and viscous:
it's last orders
and we've work to do.

Last Stop

Half man, half whisky, he staggers
the train-side one malt at a time,
slumps against the train's outer skin,
peers in to distil a view. He gets a taste
for designated seating, swaggers in.

Reservation tickets meet him:
Queensferry to Glasgow,
a return from Shotts, a window
seat through Paisley. He stumbles,
limbs splashed out to catch

himself, and like Vitruvian man
he stands sketch-still as though bound
by the will of the station. In a moment
of clarity he takes the tickets,
rips them, wild but steady,

hurls them high above the seats.
They hit the luggage hold and fall
like carriage snow. He drifts back,
sits back, lets everything rest
in his confetti.

Last Orders

Chucking out time, not quite Baltic.
You're on the edge of devastation. It's clear
through the whisky in your eyes, something
under your breath. You murmur on
about heroin and suicide, that you were
Gonna be a daddy, eh. Gonna be a daddy, eh.
Aye, a daddy, how your dad took you aside,
shook your hand; congratulations, for once.

We ask where you're going
tonight, if you've someone to see,
somewhere to stay other than under
another doorway. But we are ghosts
whose voices cannot penetrate through
the loss, and you tell us you were *gonna be*
a daddy. My dad shook my hand, aye a daddy.
It's nae-one's right tae terminate.

Tonight, she'd bought you drinks,
fed you as she sipped on water
after water (to make it easier?), told you
she didn't want to bring another bairn
to this terrible world. You ran to the toilet,
cried your eyes out, hurled.

Eventually our voices settle with your eyes
and we agree on a quiet place to think
and sleep. You've a pal a way away,
so we wait for the bus, push two pounds
into your palm for chips, tell you
It'll be okay, you're doing well
and you hold us to you, tell us
he shook my hand.

You stagger aboard, sit, your eyes still
shaken, contemplating the night
as the bus departs and you give
a vacant smile, a thumbs up and we go
back to the pub for one more.

Outside the Pub, Hurricane Bawbag

rips the street, takes mothers
off their feet, police off the beat
but as I wither with a dozen smokers
trying to catch a flame between us
a man in his seventies, half bent,
muttering, struggling but intent
pushes an empty wheelchair
up the road to the peak, stops, checks
the decline, shuffles into the seat
and lets the wind take him

A Veteran

Your first steady step is clean: a left,
left, left, right, left, your skirmish green
suit, pinned and proper, regimented red
pom-pommed beret, straight firesnap spine.

You take the seat in front of mine.
Your smoke lingers, chokes
the atmosphere and without apology
you sleeve away a silent tear.

It could be Veterans Day, it could be
another farewell ceremony. You start
a slow vibration, like a laugh building
in to the shudder of artillery and I hope

you won't look at me as you quicken
in your place. I hope your hand settles
on the trigger and your body stiffens.
You stand steady, your first step is clean.

The National Portrait Gallery

A frame to the country? Pff!
When you come to see me
you see something of me,
my fat face thinned, shaven
clean for your visit. My eyes
are not history, the lochs,
my hair has no connection
to heather, though I've smelt it.

I am a moment. A posture.
When the cleaners kill
the roaring vacuums, put out
the lights, we are all in the
death of darkness. It is only you,
who comes here and stares,
that is the portrait.

Bring the world to me, to us,
our catalogue of depiction.
We need something other
than ourselves, for your frame
to extend ours, the wind
that opens the door, the road
fumes, your whining, running
children to clear the fust
of our corridors.

In this place you hang
with us, your moment
reflecting in our painted eyes.

Remembrance

Whose mind is yours? I see
your jaw clap closed, eyes strained
with each morning. I bring you
the small relief of tea and toast.
You make a smile for a stranger.

On Sunday you shat on the kitchen floor
and blamed the cat. Its size was the giveaway,
and that you've not owned a cat in twelve years.

It's both easier and more devastating to joke
than to reveal myself, to say you're sick
rather than dying. I avoid the lounge
where you sit reminding me to check the porch
light, check the porch light, to check the porch light,
to check that I am not wanted in your house.

In youth you sold antiques, played cricket,
imported tea. The house is arranged by relic:
the unchanging glare of portraiture, framed liner
tickets to mark each year spent at sea, your captain's cap,
hand-crafted bat resting in the living room.

And in the hall you stand mesmerised
by the grandfather clock, its face watching yours,
face watching face watching face watching face
until I lay my hand on your shoulder, recognition
finding me in you for a brief moment
when I take your arm in mine
and we return together.

On Her Return from Afghanistan

My sister told me how she'd sewn
the stomachs of two boys who set off
a land mine whilst playing football near the market;
removed the overcooked
skin, tendons, muscle and cartilage
from the legs of a woman trying to save
her photos during a house fire;
administered the drugs to a man
she had eaten eggs with, knowing
his death was certain.

At my mum's wedding she was hit by a tirade of
Oh how do you do it?
smiled, told them it was a job, that she just
pulled the theatre curtain, hovered
in helicopters, let the bullets fly
as she loaded them onto the stretcher,
that you become immune, just a robot, just a doctor.

During the wedding reception we sat in the drum
of the disco and wept
because neither of us had said goodbye
to our Nan before she died.

Nan, Come from the Water

It's strange how I think of you

more often now, since we sent you

    away. Now sometimes you

are swimming in my mind, in your kitchen you

spout water from a cosie, slice moist cake, you

    wash your working, lively hands as you

hang translucent, angelic. If you

could be here I'd take you

    aside, ask to relive the times you

walked us through your wild garden, how you

plucked beans with us, cleaned with us until you

    had made a meal, a family you

could live for, good enough to eat, head high as you

emerge through us, rippling. Nan, you

    are more than just you,

you are the myth and the memory –

Backlash

	The Nose	The Mind	The Eye
My first girlfriend's foundation	Plasticine Clotted cream Unwashed towels Mace	Wolverhampton back alleys, discount gin and the trepidation of hands	A block of lavender soap held in marigolds by an attractive lady from a shopping magazine
Snow	A Fox's Glacier A Fisherman's Friend A Shot of chilled vodka Road Fumes	Waiting for the car, I fall in, ask how you're doing, chirp. We drive in the accepted peace of the radio	A gob of mouthwash in a clean porcelain sink
Love	Cherry Bakewell The debris of a firework Citrus fruits	Away from the world, a haze of cocktails and takeaways, two nocturnal	Paint hurled against a magnolia wall
The doctor's surgery	Piss Bleach Morning breath	Somewhere that I was not as you lay dying	A tortoise in a box in a shed in a garden where runner beans grow
Poetry	Chips and sauce, a gherkin Washing Powder A Sunday Roast Smoke from a blown out candle	The rattle and murmur of everything	A cosmonaut pedalling the vacuum towards their nearest star

Ghazal Jigsaw

From the small, closed window by our study table the stars are set
like the pieces of your space jigsaw. I ask if you're any closer. *The stars are set*

you mutter as you slot another nook into the realised corner, and yet
you seem unsure which cosmos you've pieced together. The stars are set

upon like foxes: your hands are hungry dogs. Your eyes are ready trumpets.
Your mind is a nebula and then *aha*, you've a northern glow and the stars are set

in their place with a satisfying *click*. Another, two more and you're a puzzle-rocket.
They look so still and steady with you, but through our study window the stars are set

in more dimensions than just those two. You drop a red dwarf and I reach for it.
You continue. I open the window and, like the sails of a ship, the stars are set.

Kiting

No angel is safe.
We fire our flimsy diamond
into the summer
night. You rush

to catch it – no not it –
its bravado, its promise
that we will never end
the flight together.
It's here to tell you

it's inevitable, as inevitable
as its string dancing
in the chaos of itself.
We'll cast that chaos
back, pick the knots out

until feathers fall
from the clouds.
Then we can build ourselves
the wings we need

to chase
that dance
into the ravel
of the night.

Hanging Out the Washing at Night

What a snail you make
pulling the ocean from a sheet
flapping it in the wind
like it was nothing. The world
unravels in your hands
as you clip clothes to the line
like stars winking
in their place, transfixed
by you in your nightie
between the shuffle of trees
and a dog's distant growl.

My eyes flicker between
the tenement shadow and
your silhouette stretching
over the bed sheets. You bend
for the final piece, your slender legs
shuddering in the chilling darkness
and I think
of that bold look you gave
before you took the night in
your empty basket
and returned to the house.

Acknowledgements

Acknowledgements are due to the editors of the following magazines and anthologies in which some of these poems, or other versions of them, first appeared:

Venture, The Genomics Forum, The Scottish Poetry Library, Drey, Inkwell, Cambridge Library, The Human Journal, New Writing Scotland, The Istanbul Review, KaffeeKlatsch, Spaces of Their Own, Octavius, Scotsman, Open Mouse, Deep Water, Amazing Stories, Poetry Planet, Best Scottish Poems, Gutter, Be The First To Like This, Revenant, Rhysling Anthology, Edinburgh Review, Caboodle, The Lumen, Prole, and *Emma Press Anthology of Age*

Huge thanks to my editor, Andrew Philip, for his advice and critical eye, helping to bring shape to this collection. Thank you to Alan Gillis and Aileen Ballantyne, who spent many hours and beverages patiently poring over my ramblings. There are many people who have seen these poems at various stages of indecency, including Colin McGuire, Mairi Campbell-Jack, Bill Herbert, Alan Jamieson, Lauren Pope, Pakkun Jones, Ryan Van Winkle, Dave Coates, Emma Sedlak and Miriam Johnson. To you all, and everyone I haven't mentioned who provided their feedback, thank you. To my publisher, Freight, and all those who sail within, thank you for your openness to my work and your efforts in bringing my poetry to print. My partner, Joanna McLaughlin, thank you – as always – for putting up with me and my annoyances/quirks. To Edwin Morgan, who unknowingly acted as my muse whilst I wrote this book, many thanks. And to all the publishers, editors, writers, events organisers, friends, foes and family who have supported or influenced my work in some way – thank you, thank you, thank you! Without you all, this book wouldn't have been possible.